GLEN HOUSE
COMMUNICATIONS

P.O. Box 64433
Los Angeles, California 90064

Library of Congress Catalogue Card Number: 84-80866

ISBN 0-918269-00-8

COVER AND BOOK DESIGN BY BRUCE BOETTCHER.

LAYOUT BY TSO.

THE TEXT TYPE IS ORACLE II.
TYPESETTING AND PASTE-UP BY MASTERFILE, SANTA MONICA, CALIFORNIA.

COLOR SEPARATIONS, PRINTING, AND BINDING WERE EXECUTED BY TOPPAN PRINTING CO., LTD., TOKYO, JAPAN.

If your bookseller is out of stock or you would like additional copies, please remit $17.95 plus $1.50 per book for mailing and handling to: GLEN HOUSE COMMUNICATIONS, P.O. Box 64433, Los Angeles, California 90064. California residents please add 6½% sales tax of $1.17 per book.

(cover painting)
LOS ANGELES AT DUSK
Like arteries carrying life through some vast body, walkways and overpasses dominate this southerly view of Flower Street from the ramp of the World Trade Center.

LOS ANGELES
with Love

PAINTINGS BY
DOROTHY RICE

PREFACE BY
RAY BRADBURY

TEXT BY
FRED PERRY

GLEN HOUSE
COMMUNICATIONS

LOS ANGELES: WHERE DID IT GO?
WHEN WILL IT ARRIVE?

A PREFACE
BY RAY BRADBURY

Los Angeles beggars description. Trying to write something new about it, is like claiming Marjorie Main was Marilyn Monroe's sister: no one would believe it.

Los Angeles is 77 towns with no center, 81 camels seeking a desert, 99 oranges in need of a navel. The imaginative list is long. But we all know that those 77 or 81 or 99 Ohio refugee camps, spotted around Southern California, lacking a magnetized pole with a single name, probably won't find it in this century. We have long-since buried that semi-desert under Colorado river water and abundances of fruit, only to have said fruit vanish under floods of concrete.

But still the symbol of the navel-less orange seems right as our city emblem. Consider:

The Spanish priests who settled us, took vows of chastity, laid only the dust.

We are named for the Queen of Angels. A virgin.

So much for civic parenting.

Sometimes, late nights, I guess us as an immense real estate scam brought off by Indians who vanished but to resurface last year with their petrol dollars and bingo parlors, out beyond Cucamonga.

All this being true, how do you pick the porcupine up?

When asked to write this Preface, I imagined myself fresh out of orchard praise or oil-slick blame. But Dorothy Rice's watercolors stopped me warm. Why *write* about L.A., I thought, when you have someone else's eyes to *look* through!?

And Dorothy Rice does have fresh eyes and her own palette. Which means a talent for making the familiar unfamiliar, younger than when last you saw it.

I must admit I came to her watercolor portfolio with some jaundice, carrying with me the prejudice of having arrived in Los Angeles fifty years ago this week.

My dad, seeking work in the Great Depression, brought my mom, my brother Skip, and myself West with fifty bucks in his pocket to keep and feed us for six weeks. Arriving, aged 13, I ran amok on my rollerskates. The teeming cinema jungle of limousine moguls and maidens smelling of Ben Hur perfume, 5 cents a squirt, waited out there.

For months, I never stopped rolling. I skated from my apartment at Pico and Western out to ricochet off Paramount's studio gates, then carom from RKO to

Columbia, the Brown Derby, Grauman's Chinese and back, a fury after the famous, a fever on cheap wheels. I was there the day they laid the cornerstone for NBC's network station. I was there with my skates in the rain that summer night in 1934 when they premiered DAMES at the old Warner Bros. theatre. I watched a score of stars sink to their ankles in concrete in the Chinese forecourt. Between times, I hiked up to the Hollywood hills sign, loitered around famous star homes, and rode the Santa Monica pier carousel. I did it *all*.

I mention all this because fifty years later, minus rollerskates, but armed with an eye for detail and a full color-brush, Dorothy Rice has lingered in most of the same places and come away with similar remembrance. It almost seems that very little has changed.

Glance through. There's hardly a scene here I haven't lived in or visited. I have body surfed off the Santa Monica beach in the long summers of '34 and '35. I have lived with my wife Maggie and our first born, Susan, in Venice, back in the years when living there was out of poverty's necessity, not well-to-do's caprice. I have wandered in and out of the Bradbury building wishing it were mine and not some distant rich relative's. I raised, read, and educated myself to graduate from the big downtown library you will find watercolored here.

I have lived in a tenement on Temple Street, with my Chicano/Filipino friends who taught me to wear the grand summer ice cream suit. And looking once again at Rice's illustration of the Paramount Studio facade, I feel she should have painted my ghost to the right of the gate. There is where I stood for years with my camera and autograph book, waiting for Claudette Colbert or Marlene Dietrich to come steal me away.

So, to say that I am now prejudiced in favor of Dorothy Rice's recollections of a shared past which is still present, is a modest understatement indeed.

I was there. I still am. Imagine as you study each watercolor that just one second ago I flashed by on my skates. Or that, ten seconds from now, I will *arrive*. You won't be wrong.

But, while you're waiting, turn the pages. Look. Enjoy.

RAY BRADBURY
Los Angeles, Calif.
April 10, 1984

LOS ANGELES

DOROTHY CHANDLER PAVILLION
This theatre is the centerpiece of the Music Center. Jacques Lipchitz's sculpture "Peace on Earth," rises from the fountain.

HARBOR FREEWAY
Viewed from the nineteenth floor of the Arco Towers, this busy thoroughfare is travelled by half a million vehicles a day.

LOS ANGELES

It has been said that Los Angeles is more than a place on a map; it is a state of mind. For unlike cities which conjure up concrete mental pictures — San Francisco, London, New York — Los Angeles is a vast collage, its seemingly unrelated images, when viewed in proper perspective, somehow creating a unified and attractive picture. The sheer size of this behemoth community makes it one of a kind. Bordered by coastline, mountains, and desert, the city limits cover 465 square miles.

But a city is more than geographical boundaries. It is its people. And the life styles and customs of its people give each city a unique personality. Los Angeles, with its rich ethnic, and multi-cultural heritage, possesses a singularly distinct personality. Since World War II the diversity of nationalities moving into Southern California has skyrocketed. There are more languages spoken in Los Angeles than in any other city in the United States. It is truly the melting pot of America. Some have called Los Angeles the Ellis Island of the West Coast.

From its birth as a tiny Spanish outpost in the 1700s, to the sprawling international city it is today, Los Angeles has been in the process of "becoming"; a city of contrasts where the past and present coexist comfortably, their relationship loose and symbiotic. In the heart of downtown, modern high-rise buildings stand guard over historical and cultural landmarks.

Olvera Street, near the site of the original settlement — "El Pueblo de Nuestra Senora la Reina de Los Angeles" — has been preserved as it was in the eighteenth century; its open-air cafes, shops, and strolling mariachi musicians serving as ongoing reminders of the city's Spanish heritage. Nearby, Mexican-style wall murals beautify Boyle Heights in the barrio, Los Angeles' thriving Latino community. A few blocks away the aromas of stir-fried foods and incense drift past pagoda-style buildings in Chinatown, and Buddhist temples and rooftop gardens from Little Tokyo, adjacent to the civic center. The University of Southern California, the oldest and largest private university in the West, lies to the south near Exposition Park, where museums house ancient relics and contemporary scientific discoveries. A short distance from the glass towers of the financial section, Victorian and Queen Anne-style homes share neighborhoods with Tudor and Spanish-style residences. The spires of the Watts Towers identify the predominantly Black community just south of the business district. A few miles northeast, Highland Park serves as a living calendar of Los Angeles, abundant with historical homes and mission-style structures. Funky, new-wave boutiques and specialty shops add color and new life to an old section of Melrose Avenue. Hancock Park's primordial La Brea Tar Pits occupy space with the chic Los Angeles County Museum of Art. And tiny hot dog stands and burger joints do business amidst the elite eateries on La Cienega's restaurant row. Nearby, a large Jewish population occupies the Fairfax District. Southwest is Korea Town, boasting the largest Korean population outside of Korea. A wealth of other nationalities are part of the bountiful cultural mixture, each one distinct, yet connected to the whole that is Los Angeles.

Modern domiciles of affluence — Beverly Hills, Bel Air, Brentwood, Marina del Rey, Pacific Palisades and Malibu — counterpoint locales which ring of the Old West: Stone Canyon, Atwater, Eagle Rock, and Coldwater Canyon. Cal Tech, Griffith Observatory, and the Jet Propulsion Laboratory celebrate the quest for the future, while Romanesque sports palaces like the Olympic Auditorium, The Forum, Dodger Stadium, and the Coliseum maintain Man's ancient attachment to physical competition. Los Angeles is a city with many hearts, each pumping life into one vast body.

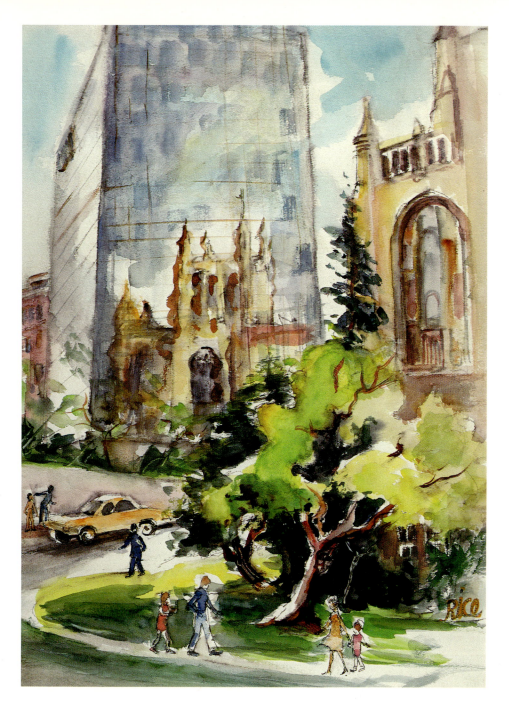

REFLECTION OF THE FIRST CONGREGATIONAL CHURCH
Shimmering on the wall of a modern glass tower, this Gothic church near Lafeyette Park contains the largest pipe organ west of the Mississippi. Lloyd C. Douglas, author of ''The Robe,'' was its minister from 1926 to 1929.

Five miles to the west of downtown Los Angeles there is a community stretching along the base of the foothills. Even if one were unfamiliar with Southern California, it would be easy to locate this spot. For perched on the hills high above the city, there is an immense sign which is visible for miles, its towering letters spelling out one word: HOLLYWOOD.

West of downtown Los Angeles lies a fertile land of mansions, tennis courts and pools, manicured lawns and pedicured poodles, Rolls Royces and street signs which read: NO OVERNIGHT PARKING. This is the land that movies built. This is Beverly Hills. Adjacent to Beverly Hills is Century City, the most impressive assortment of modern high-rise office buildings in Los Angeles. Intersecting Century City and Beverly Hills is Wilshire Boulevard, a broad, bustling thoroughfare extending from downtown Los Angeles, west to the coast; passing through places like the Miracle Mile District, and the Wilshire Corridor. Lined by high-priced, high-rise residences, this area has been nicknamed "Condominium Canyon."

Further west, at the edge of the continental United States, are the domains of leisure and easy living; the beach towns. Santa Monica, Pacific Palisades, Malibu, Marina del Rey, Playa del Rey, Venice, Manhattan, Zuma, Hermosa, and Redondo Beaches.

To the northeast of Los Angeles, nestled against the foot of the San Gabriel Mountains, is Pasadena, home of the internationally renowned Norton Simon Museum of Art, splendid historical homes, and the Tournament of Roses Parade. And east of Pasadena is Arcadia, site of the Arboretum, a one hundred and twenty-seven acre botanical paradise, with lakes, waterfalls, and historic buildings. Nearby is the Santa Anita Race Track, a lightning-fast oval navigated by top, thoroughbred winners.

The rich heritage of Los Angeles lives in its vast array of historical landmarks, architectural structures, and most vividly, in the life styles of its people. Blessed with an ideal climate, room to breathe, and a cultural diversity unequaled anywhere, the City of Angels is truly the "International City" of today.

MILLION DOLLAR THEATRE
This Spanish-baroque style theatre, one of the first movie palaces in the country, adds an 18th-century flavor to the rich Mexican atmosphere of South Broadway.

BILTMORE HOTEL
Opened in 1923, the thousand-room Biltmore was declared an historical landmark in 1969. Located on Pershing Square, this opulent hotel possesses the grandeur and elegance of European Palaces.

LITTLE TOKYO ◄
The cultural heart of the city's bustling Japanese community, jammed with shops and restaurants, and the new Otani Hotel.

GRIFFITH OBSERVATORY
Situated on a hilltop high above the nation's largest municipal park, the tri-domed, art-deco observatory is visited by crowds who come to gaze at the heavens through the powerful twelve-inch telescope, or to watch dazzling laserium shows in the domed theatre.

BONAVENTURE HOTEL ▶
Five gleaming cylindrical towers thrust from 5th Street like cosmic shrines; the futuristic effect enhanced by exterior elevators and the Calder sculpture in the foreground.

Rice

PANTRY CAFE

This 24-hour-a-day eaterie has been doing non-stop business since it opened during the depression. It has never been closed. Lines gather around the clock to wait for tables at this popular spot on 9th Street and Figueroa.

CITY HALL, SEEN FROM LITTLE TOKYO ▶

Completed in 1928, this twenty eight-story "Italian Classic" building was the tallest structure in Los Angeles until the mid-sixties when prohibitive building restrictions were relaxed.

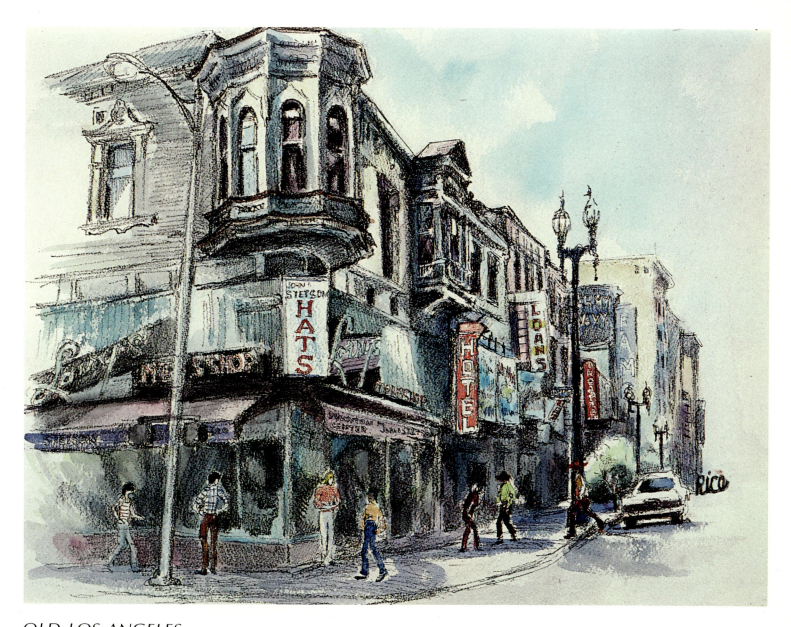

OLD LOS ANGELES
Turn-of-the-century architecture still stands on 5th and Main Streets.

CENTRAL LIBRARY ON HOPE STREET ◄
Comprised of Byzantine, Islamic, Mediterranean and Egyptian forms, the library graphically symbolizes the melding of cultures and styles in Los Angeles. Interior and exterior sculptures by Lee Lawrie, and huge murals by Dean Cornwall enhance the distinct beauty of this landmark built in 1926.

OLVERA STREET

Preserved today as a ''typical Mexican market place,'' this short, but bustling street marks the birthplace of Los Angeles; its colorful shops, stalls, and restaurants celebrating the city's rich Mexican heritage.

CHINATOWN
Built by Chinese settlers during the California gold rush, some of these pagoda-style, brick buildings date back to the 1870s. Ornate, 30-foot-high wall murals with dragons and warriors decorate this community.

ARCO TOWERS
Massive twin towers jut fifty-two stories skyward from the Atlantic Richfield Plaza on South Flower Street. Forty feet below street level, more than fifty shops and restaurants do business in a spacious subterranean mall.

AUTOMOBILE CLUB OF SOUTHERN CALIFORNIA
The club promotes motoring and sightseeing in the wide-open West through magazines and tourist maps. Its Spanish Colonial-style headquarters were built in 1923.

OLYMPIC AUDITORIUM
Known for its wild and colorful professional wrestling matches, the Olympic draws huge, boisterous crowds, who come to cheer for the good guys.

COCA COLA BOTTLING COMPANY ◄
Built in 1941 to resemble a ship, it is complete with portholes, cargo doors, and a catwalk.

 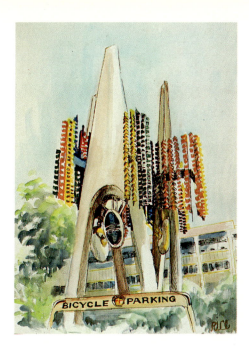 

BRADBURY BUILDING
This incredible five-story structure, with its skylighted atrium, wrought-iron staircases, marble stairs, and open-cage elevators, celebrates the architectural artistry of the late 19th century in the heart of "Old Downtown."

TRIFORIUM
The sixty-foot-tall Triforium is an audacious, off-beat sculpture on the Los Angeles Mall. It produces light shows with electronic music.

UNION STATION
Trains arrive as they have since 1939 at this impressive, Mediterranean-style terminal. Built through combined resources of the Union Pacific, Santa Fe, and Southern Pacific railroads, the structure stands as the "Last of the Great Terminals."

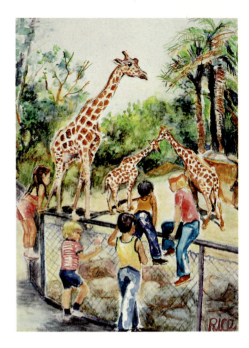

GIRAFFES

LOS ANGELES ZOO
Covering the eastern portion of Griffith Park's 4,000 acres, the Los Angeles Zoo houses some of the most exotic animals in captivity.

TRAVELTOWN IN GRIFFITH PARK
A collection of antique locomotives create a nostalgic journey into the railroad's past.

SANTA MONICA

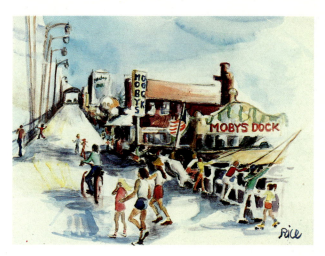

MOBY'S DOCK
Resembling a New England wharfside pub,
Moby's Dock on the Santa Monica Pier offers
a panoramic view of the bay.

SANTA MONICA PIER
One of the oldest carrousels in the nation stands at the pier's entrance, where turn-of-the-century trolley cars once stopped. A Mediterranean-style promenade passes beneath the pier.

SANTA MONICA

From its beginnings, when a few homes dotted the area at the exit of Santa Monica Canyon, to the flourishing leisure community it is today, Santa Monica has been blessed with clean air, and with the exception of infrequent winter storms, ideal, year round weather. Perched high on a mesa overlooking the Pacific, the view is picture-postcard spectacular.

Yachts and fishing boats, escorted by dolphins and migrating whales, cruise past the breakwater of the bay. Sailboats, their jibs billowing, tack in the wind. Catalina Island juts hypnotically out of the ocean thirty miles west. And north, clinging to the edge of the mainland, the affluent homes of Malibu loom over the beaches; tides and occasional storm seas washing at their foundations.

Directly below the mesa, extending over the bay, is the Santa Monica Pier, a turn of the century landmark which was the end of the old trolley line from Los Angeles. Nearly torn down for development in 1973, this site was saved from extinction by community pride and determination. Its restaurants, shops, rides, and colorful arcades draw large crowds. And calliope music from one of the oldest carrousels in the United States toots out a greeting at the pier's entrance on Ocean Avenue. Passing beneath the pier is a wide, Mediterranean-style promenade; a pedestrian-only walk lined by towering palm trees, food stands, volleyball courts, gymnastic bars, surfboard and skate rental shops, and "Muscle Beach," a plot of sand where statuesque bodybuilders — male and female — pump iron, pose, and draw crowds. Throughout the year the beach of Santa Monica is abundant with picnickers, surfers, joggers, strollers, and those who just want to "catch some rays."

In addition to the merry-go-round on the pier, there are restaurants, a fresh fish market, and a bait and tackle shop. Fishermen gather at the end of the pier to drop lines and crab nets, and a busy boat rental shack keeps the bay dotted with small craft. A pinball arcade, skeeball, dart booths, bumper cars, and even a fortune teller add a festive carnival atmosphere to this popular gathering place.

South of the pier, running parallel to Ocean Avenue, is Main Street. For many years, low-rent shops and cafes in disrepair lined this short strip of real estate, and were hangouts for beach people and Bohemian types. No longer. In recent years, posh restaurants, galleries, and antique shops have claimed the territory; turning Main Street into "Rodeo Drive West."

ARRIVING AT THE SANTA MONICA PIER
A wide archway greets visitors at the Ocean Avenue entrance to the pier.

HIGH VIEW OF SANTA MONICA
Overlooking the Pacific Coast Highway north of the Santa Monica Pier, a walkway spirals across the busy highway from the mesa down to seaside homes and private clubs along the beach.

SANTA MONICA IN SEPTEMBER
The hottest month of the year draws crowds to the beach like a magnet. The temperature at water's edge is often fifteen to twenty degrees cooler than inland.

VENICE CANALS
Gondolas once glided through these backwaters.

VENICE

The promenade in Santa Monica leads south to Venice Beach, a funky, laid-back, stream-of-consciousness community. Originally designed as a dream city in the style of Venice, Italy, it was replete with canals, bridges, and gondolas. The discovery of oil blew the dream apart. The petroleum industry consumed the land until the wells were depleted. The town eventually became a haven for free-thinkers, poets, and artists. Its smooth promenade has made it the outdoor roller skating capital of the United States. Four of the original canals remain today. Navigated by residents in row boats, and serving as home to large populations of ducks and geese, these backwaters make Venice the most unusual beach community in Southern California.

MARINA del REY
and
THE BEACHES

Adjoining Venice to the south is the center of the "singles scene" in Southern California; Marina del Rey. A plethora of high-rent apartments, condos, and nightclubs surround the largest man-made boat harbor in the world. Plentifully stocked with yachts, bikini-clad sunbunnies, and bronze adonises, the Marina is contemporary, hip, and expensive.

Further south, the warm sands of Playa del Rey, Manhattan Beach, and Redondo Beach are visited ritually by sunbathers, surfers, volleyball fanatics, body builders, scuba divers, and fishermen. The ultra-chic community of Palos Verdes blankets a fifteen mile stretch of verdant headland above the Pacific, where sprawling estates with bridle paths and stables, are home to thoroughbreds and quarter horses.

And to the north, just beyond Santa Monica, where the Pacific Palisades meets Malibu, is the J. Paul Getty Museum, a re-creation of an ancient Roman country villa, which contains one of the most important art collections in the United States.

Hugging the coastline in Malibu, is the exclusive "Movie Colony," where show-biz personalities, free from the onslaught of fans and autograph hounds, can lead normal lives.

BEACH SCENE
A typical day at water's edge.

SKATEBOARDS IN VENICE BEACH
Joggers, skaters, and bicyclers make for busy traffic along the promenade near the Venice pier.

PACIFIC PALISADES
Distinctive homes occupy this lush, hillside community overlooking the Pacific, just north of Santa Monica.

PALOS VERDES
Rimmed by a fifteen mile scenic drive, the beach here is as exclusive as its posh community, not far from the Los Angeles International Airport.

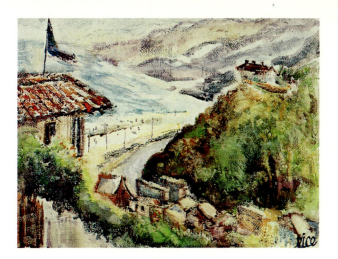

VIEW OF THE OCEAN
The Pacific Coast Highway winds gently along the coastline towards Malibu to the north.

MERRY-GO-ROUND
Residing on the Santa Monica Pier, forty-three colorful wooden horses have been making their circular trips for nearly a hundred years in this carrousel, which was seen in the film, ''The Sting.''

PARADISE COVE
Privacy is the key attraction at this beautiful, secluded beach. Its clear waters are paradise for swimmers and surfers.

MARINA DEL REY BEACH
Sleek, tan bodies soak up sun on the beach, and patrons, sitting at the windows of bayside restaurants, watch sailboats race and windsurfers cut across the glassy bay.

MALIBU PIER
Offering a spectacular coastline view, this structure is dominated by the seafood stand and bait shop at the end of the pier. Deep sea fishing boats do heavy business here, and water taxies make the short trip between the Santa Monica and Malibu piers.

SKATE RENTALS IN VENICE
Skaters congregate in front of the arcade to show off.

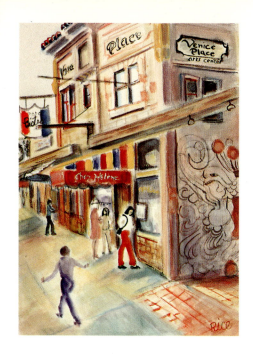  

VENICE PLACE
These remodeled older buildings house antique and art shops, cafes, and boutiques.

PLAYA DEL REY
As if daring nature to test their structural integrity, these homes cling precariously to the high bluffs above Playa del Rey, just south of the Marina.

CANASTA ON OCEAN AVENUE
Attracted by the balmy pacific breeze, towering palm trees, and cool, well-trimmed lawns, groups of retirees gather to test their canasta and chess prowess at the tables on Ocean Avenue.

SURFING IN MANHATTAN BEACH
Surfers plod beachward past renovated Victorian-style homes near the Manhattan Beach pier. Blessed with ideal surfing conditions, this community south of the Marina draws thousands of water sports enthusiasts throughout the year.

FISHERMAN'S VILLAGE IN MARINA DEL REY ◄
Waterfront stores and restaurants with panoramic views of the bay, make this Fiji Way locale the shopping and eating center of the Marina.

BEVERLY HILLS

BEVERLY WILSHIRE HOTEL COURTYARD
Framed by massive Louis XV gates, the main entrance is illuminated at night by gaslights imported from Edinburgh Castle in Scotland.

BEVERLY HILLS

From the manicured parks and storybook mansions of its residential area, to its high-rent business district, nothing is remotely commonplace about Beverly Hills. Multi-million dollar homes with swimming pools, tennis courts, gyms and saunas, are surrounded by palatial walls and private entrance gates manned by uniformed guards. The Beverly Hills school system has one of the best reputations in the nation. Well-off families migrate here in droves to expose their little ones to the finest education available. Rolls Royces, Jaguars, and Mercedes now roam this plot of land, once the domain of plow horses and orange groves. The Beverly Hills Hotel — situated on twelve hillside acres of garden estate — reveals the unique affluence of this community. Unlike hotels ''looking to do business'' this playground for the well-to-do does not accept conventions. Even the wearing of name tags is a no-no. Beverly Hills boasts of other lovely hotels; the Beverly Wilshire, Beverly Hilton, L'Ermitage, Beverly Rodeo, Beverly Crest and Holiday Inn.

Between Wilshire and Santa Monica Boulevards lies the mecca of West Coast chic. The names read like a Who's Who of internationally known merchants — Hermès, Fred, Cartier, Van Cleef & Arpels, Lanvin, Ted Lapidus, Saint Laurent, Battaglia, Céline, Courrèges, Bijan, Carroll & Company, Giorgio, Elizabeth Arden, Nina Ricci, Caritta, Louis Vuitton,

ROBINSON'S DEPARTMENT STORE ◄
Completed in 1952, this impressive structure on Wilshire Boulevard is the centerpiece for twenty other Robinson's, located between Santa Barbara and San Diego. The first Robinson's Store opened for business in 1883.

Jerry Magnin and Gucci — pop out everywhere along Rodeo Drive; probably the only street in the world with its own public relations firm. Here are shops, restaurants, and galleries, whose leases alone are worth small fortunes. Here, one can browse through boutiques while sipping exotic drinks prepared by on-duty bartenders, or shoot a leisurely game of billiards, while a tailor makes adjustments on just-purchased, designer clothes.

Nearby are other luxurious shopping palaces like I. Magnin, Gumps, Bonwit Teller, Saks, Robinson's, Neiman Marcus, Abercrombie & Fitch, Tiffany & Company, Grand Passage, Number One Rodeo Drive, and Rodeo Collection.

Fashionable Beverly Hills housewives, secretaries, businessmen, girls in tennis outfits, and well known movie and television stars, window shop and stroll the sidewalks. Several different languages drift through the air, adding an international flavor to the scene.

Some very elegant restaurants are found in Beverly Hills, and when the weather is beautiful, which is most of the year, luncheon alfresco at the Bistro Garden, Pastel, Cafe Rodeo, Cafe Swiss, the Daisy, Cafe Casino and the Polo Lounge patio are favorite spots to catch the passing scene.

Beverly Hills is a powerful celebration of success and easy living. And its success hangs loose and comfortable, like a well-worn yet elegant piece of clothing.

RODEO DRIVE

The tasteful architecture, and easy going atmosphere evident along this short strip of land, mask some of the highest priced real estate — per inch — in the world. The elegant Beverly Wilshire Hotel dominates the background on Wilshire Boulevard.

POOL AT THE BEVERLY HILLS HOTEL

The pool of "The Pink Palace" along with the hotel's Polo Lounge, is where show-biz personalities congregate to talk shop, take meetings, and be noticed.

GINGERBREAD HOUSE ►

Originally built as a movie set, this Hansel and Gretel home on Walden Drive stands amidst more contemporary and conventional houses; its storybook design adding a bit of fantasy to the neighborhood.

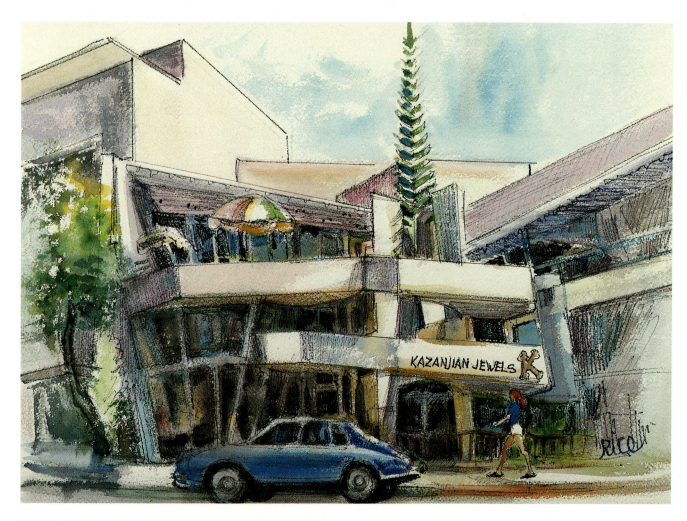

FRANK LLOYD WRIGHT BUILDING
The architecture of this Rodeo Drive structure says it all.

BEL AIR HOTEL ◄
Surrounded by lush gardens and towering palm trees, the quiet elegance of this exclusive inn, adjacent to Beverly Hills, is further enhanced by white swans who live in the hotel's pond.

WESTWOOD MOVIE THEATRES
Opening nights and exclusive engagements create lines around the block in this community next to U.C.L.A.

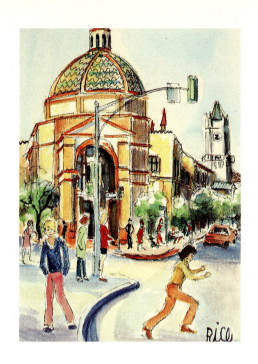 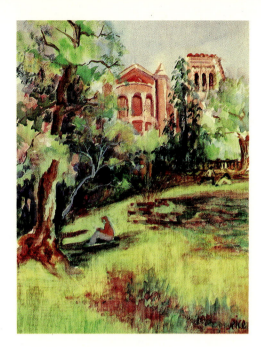 

WESTWOOD

Known simply as the village, this community adjacent to the U.C.L.A. campus, is abundant with movie theatres, trendy shops, elegant restaurants, and a cosmopolitan ambience similar to New York's upper East Side.

BEATING THE LIGHTS IN WESTWOOD
The dome of the Glendale Federal Bank Building overlooks a busy Westwood intersection. Constructed in 1929, it was one of the first buildings in the area and was visible for miles.

U.C.L.A. CAMPUS
This mammoth campus contains beautiful sculpture, botanical gardens, and vast lawns.

JANSS DRUGSTORE
Another landmark built in 1929, now housing shops, this Mediterranean-style structure stands as a reminder of simpler times.

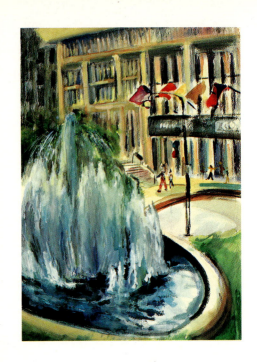 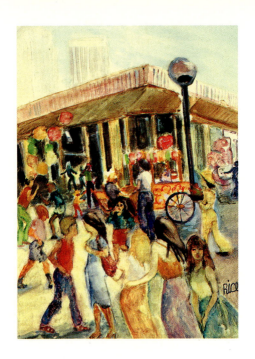 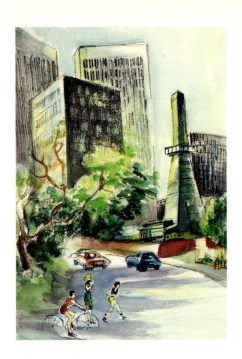

CENTURY CITY

Monolithic office buildings thrust skyward from what was once the back lot of 20th Century Fox Studios. A street sign on one of the main boulevards says a lot about its show-biz past: AVENUE OF THE STARS.

THE FOUNTAIN
A large fountain on Avenue of the Stars is the focal point between the ABC Entertainment Center — a modern complex of theatres, shops, and restaurants — and the Century Plaza Hotel.

CENTURY CITY SHOPPING CENTER
Bullocks, Joseph Magnin, The Broadway, and many other stores, make this a favorite shopping mall.

CENTURY CITY, SEEN FROM OLYMPIC BOULEVARD
An oil derrick near the Twin Towers in the heart of Century City, pumps riches from the earth as it has for decades.

HELLO DOLLY
The movie set on the lot of 20th Century Fox Studios.

HOLLYWOOD

MAGIC CASTLE

MANN'S CHINESE THEATRE
Originally built by Sid Grauman in the halcyon days of Hollywood,
the cement slabs on the floor of its courtyard are covered with
handprints and footprints of the stars.

HOLLYWOOD

When Hollywood was in its infancy, when the first two-reeler Westerns were being cranked out, there was a dust-choked clod of land on what is now Sunset Boulevard. This place was called Gower Gulch. Cowboys would ride into town looking for work in the new-fangled movies. There were no stuntmen back then. These guys were the real thing. They got payed a day's wage for doing what they did best; Roping, riding, and fighting. On camera. And many was the time, after a long day, that a couple of the boys would overindulge in Red Eye at the saloon in Gower Gulch, and a gunfight would break out. Numerous dead cowboys silently attested to the fact that Hollywood was no tinseltown back then. Everything was real after work. Even the bullets.

At the turn of the century, when Hollywood was a sleepy agricultural community, a new industry erupted into existence in New York; the MOVIES. Because of patent restrictions imposed on the film making machines back east, producers stampeded west and set up shop in Southern California. A power structure was quickly established. Composed of producers, actors, directors and writers, this new royalty laid claim to the territory. Hollywood became a boom town, its land devoured by studios, theatres, and mansions. Aided by a well-oiled publicity machine, actors and actresses were groomed, molded, then catapulted to fame. The star system had been born.

Hollywood thrives today as the hub of the entertainment business, its glories — past and present — etched into its very architecture. Large bronze stars, commemorating film, television, radio, and recording personalities, are imbedded along the sidewalks of Hollywood

Boulevard. The Egyptian, and Mann's Chinese theatres loom up on Hollywood Boulevard, audacious monuments to the boom town heyday of the movies. And built into the contour of the hills just north, is the Hollywood Bowl, a gigantic amphitheatre, where open-air concerts and shows pack in more than seventeen thousand people a performance.

Mulholland Drive, the renounded hillside thoroughfare, winds its way through the northern, residential area of the Hollywood Hills leading to the stylish homes in Nichols and Laurel Canyons, some of which once belonged to early Hollywood movie stars.

Sprawling across the slopes of the Hollywood Hills, Forest Lawn Memorial Park contains a variety of churches, and parishes with beautiful mosaics and paintings, and vast areas of landscaped greenery. Life-size figures of film stars and famous personalities, striking well-known poses, take up residence in the Hollywood Wax Museum. And the fifty-foot high Hollywood sign, erected by developers in 1923, towers above the Los Angeles basin from the summit of Mount Lee.

Since its first two-reeler Westerns were cranked out on dusty farms, Hollywood has been celebrating its own, ''bigger than life'' personality; a vigorous image which has been shouted, not whispered across the globe.

ROAD TO THE MAGIC CASTLE ►
Once a private Hollywood Hills residence, this fairytale structure was turned into a ''members only'' nightclub for renowned magicians to exchange tricks of the trade.

CINERAMA DOME
Surround-Sound, Dolby stereo, and a gigantic screen, make this theatre on Sunset Boulevard ideal for watching mega-bucks, special effects movies.

CAPITOL RECORDS BUILDING ▶
Looking like a huge stack of records on Hollywood and Vine, the building is an architectural advertisement for the recording industry.

PANTAGES THEATRE ◀
One of the first art-deco movie palaces in the nation, this opulent Hollywood Boulevard theatre seats more than two thousand people. In 1977 it was converted to live theatre.

THE MOVIE STUDIOS

From their birth as tiny, seat-of-the-pants operations on farms and chicken ranches, to their zenith, when gargantuan sound stages and back lots possessed the land, the studios had become firmly entrenched in the public's imagination. Scaled-down replicas of mountain ranges, jungles, raging oceans, and entire towns, covered back lots from Culver City to the San Fernando Valley.

20th Century Fox Studios was once so vast, that when it sold a portion of its back lot to a developer in 1960, an entire business community was built there. Century City.

MGM, a gigantic walled studio, lies just south of 20th Century Fox in Culver City. Through its gates in the heyday of the 30s, 40s, and 50s, walked "more stars than there are in the heavens."

Paramount Studios occupies a huge piece of land on Melrose Avenue in Hollywood.

Columbia and Warner Bros. Studios share space on the sprawling, Burbank Studios lot in the San Fernando Valley. And nearby, are the Walt Disney Studios.

Universal Studios dominate the southern end of the Cahuenga Pass above North Hollywood. Universal Studios is the largest studio in the world. So large, that its public tours are conducted from trams. So large, it is now called Universal City, complete with hotels, shops, restaurants, and an outdoor amphitheatre.

Hollywood is the film, television, radio, and recording capital of the world.

GATES OF PARAMOUNT PICTURES
Its original main gate is well recognized from the film "Sunset Boulevard."

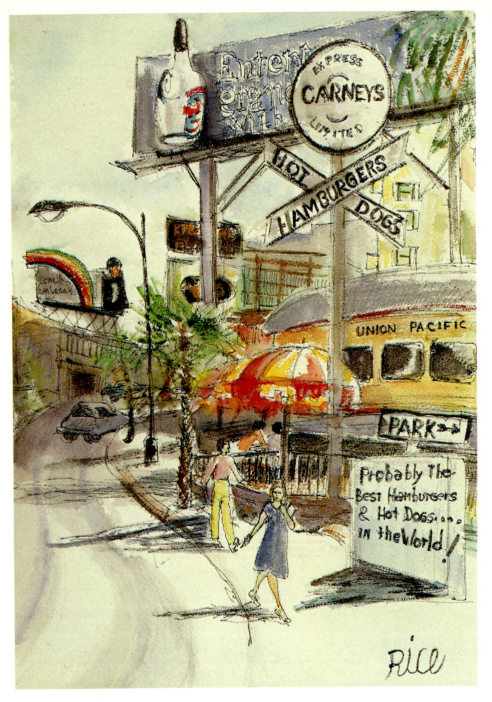

SUNSET STRIP

Armies of towering billboards line this section of Sunset Boulevard. Clubs, discos, and restaurants make the ''strip'' the hottest night spot in Los Angeles.

TOWER RECORDS

GAZZARIES ON THE STRIP

FARMER'S MARKET

Four decades ago, a few farmers started gathering on a field to sell their produce from the backs of trucks. Today, modern produce stalls, open-air restaurants, bakeries, and shops occupy this land on Fairfax Avenue.

LOOKOUT MOUNTAIN

This scenic spot just off Laurel Canyon Boulevard offers a panoramic view of the Los Angeles basin.

POINTS OF VIEW

BONNIE BRAE HOUSE
Handsome Queen Anne-style residences dominate the 1890's architecture on Bonnie Brae Street.

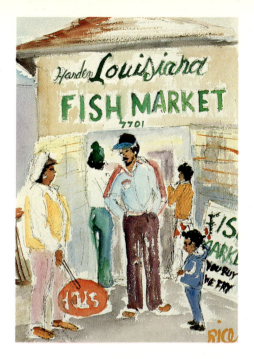

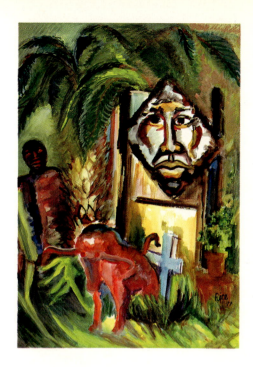

LOUISIANA FISH MARKET
A touch of the South on Hoover Street enhances the rich ethnic heritage of South Central Los Angeles.

UNIVERSAL MISSION
The brotherhood of all men is celebrated from the pulpit of this mission-style church on Hoover Street in South Central Los Angeles.

ST. ELMO'S VILLAGE
This cluster of houses was transformed from run-down bungalows into a living mural by black artist Rozell Sykes in 1961. The village, located on St. Elmo Drive near Venice and La Brea Boulevard is now a community for black artists.

WATTS TOWERS ◄
Simon Rodia, an Italian immigrant, spent thirty-three years between 1924 and 1951, constructing his monument to the human spirit. Created from steel reinforcing rods, broken tiles, and odds and ends, its three conical towers rise from Watts, South Central Los Angeles' predominantly black community.

BOYLE HEIGHTS

CHANGING TIMES
This unique Boyle Heights church graphically symbolizes the melding of religious philosophies and cultures in Los Angeles.

BROOKLYN AVENUE IN JUNE ▶
On a warm Sunday, a Chicano wedding gets underway inside this old Brooklyn Avenue movie theatre in the heart of the barrio.

LUMMIS HOUSE
The "Rock House" on Avenue 43 in Highland Park was built by Charles Lummis — first City Editor of the Los Angeles Times — and one Indian assistant. Completed in 1910, the structure is comprised entirely of boulders from a nearby dry river bed.

SOUTHWEST MUSEUM
Built in 1912, the museum is known throughout the World for its collection of Southwest art and Indian artifacts, some of which date back ten thousand years.

HIGHLAND PARK MURALS
Mexican-style wall murals add a colorful touch of hispanic history and culture to numerous buildings in Highland Park, just northeast of downtown Los Angeles.

HALE HOUSE
A spectacular example of the late Victorian period, this ten-room home, along with other restored houses, occupies Heritage Square, an area developed as a show place of the Victorian and early 20th century era of Los Angeles.

WILL ROGERS' HOME
An impressive collection of Will Rogers' memorabilia and Charles Russel's western paintings adorn the interior of this rustic residence. Complete with horse stables and polo field, it is now part of the Will Rogers State Historic Park, located above Pacific Palisades.

HUNTINGTON LIBRARY AND BOTANICAL GARDENS
Twelve elaborate gardens with nine thousand varieties of plants from every continent, beautify two hundred acres near Pasadena. The library houses a priceless collection of rare books and manuscripts. The art gallery is home to Gainsborough's famous ''Blue Boy'' painting.

MACARTHUR PARK
This thirty-two acre subtropical oasis was renamed in 1942 when Douglas MacArthur was at the height of his popularity. The park, located on Wilshire Boulevard near downtown Los Angeles, contains a lake for paddle boating, picnic areas, and a pavillion for band concerts.

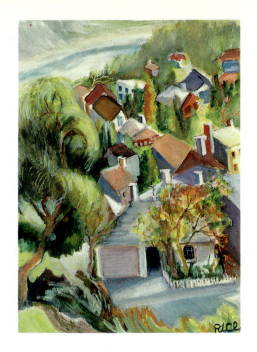  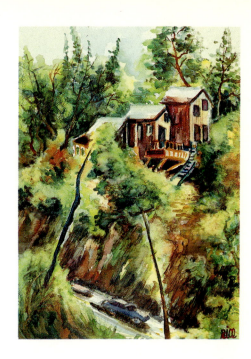

SILVERLAKE DISTRICT
A panoramic view from the hills reveals European-style homes, designed by Viennese architects Richard Neutra and S.M. Schindler.

PICNIC IN ECHO PARK
Lilies and hundreds of majestic palm trees augment the quiet beauty of this man-made lake in the hills near downtown Los Angeles.

COLDWATER CANYON
Distinctive houses inhabit the hillsides of this winding link between the Beverly Hills Hotel on Sunset Boulevard, and Ventura Boulevard in the San Fernando Valley.

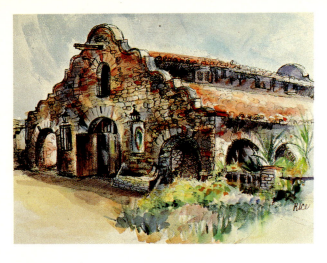

CANOGA PARK MISSION
Once a stop-off for trail weary stagecoach travelers journeying between Los Angeles and Santa Barbara, this old adobe mission in the San Fernando Valley now houses an art gallery, which features works by Mexican and American artists.

DOMICILLARY CHAPEL
Constructed in 1900 on the grounds of the Veterans Administration, this beautiful building on Wilshire Boulevard is one of the few Victorian-era structures still standing in West Los Angeles.

PACIFIC DESIGN CENTER
Built in 1975, this hulking structure was nicknamed "The Blue Whale" though closer in appearance to a blimp hanger. Located on Melrose Avenue, shops and businesses occupy its vast interior.

NUDIES IN THE VALLEY

Country music stars and modern-day cowboys shop for the latest in Western fashion at this hip, San Fernando Valley shop.

QUEEN ANNE COTTAGE

This ornate, period house was the central setting for the "Fantasy Island" television series, and is situated in the Los Angeles State and County Arboretum in Arcadia.

TRACK AT U.C.L.A.

Used by well known athletes and "civilian" joggers alike, the quarter mile oval on the U.C.L.A. campus boasts one of the finest composition surfaces in the nation.

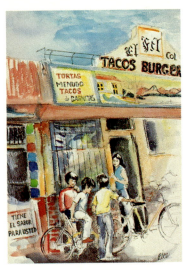

LOYOLA THEATRE ▶
An art deco movie palace is now an office building near the Los Angeles International Airport, in Westchester.

TACOS ON FIRST AVENUE ◀
The pungent aromas of menudo, chorizo, refried beans, and fresh tortillas drift through the barrio in Boyle Heights.

TAIL OF THE PUP ▼
Looking like a monster hot dog, this 1950's stand does brisk business on La Cienega's restaurant row.

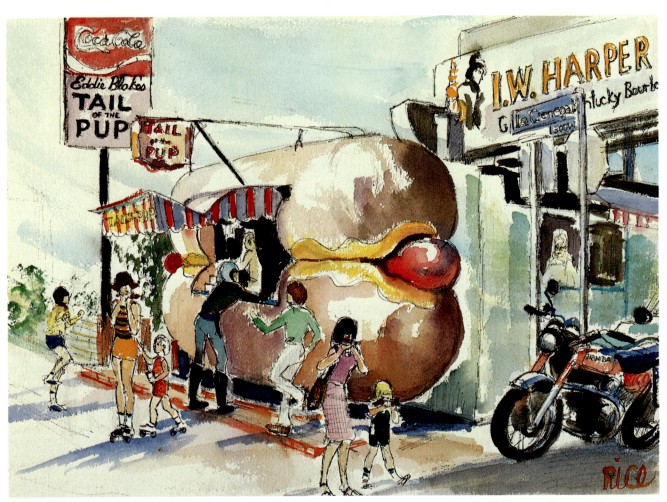

CARROLL AVENUE HOUSES
Within view of downtown, these restored homes in Angelino Heights are one of the finest collection of Victorian structures in Los Angeles.

LA BREA TAR PITS
Huge models of mastodons go down for the count in this primordial graveyard, preserved as a landmark in Hancock Park on Wilshire Boulevard.

THE TOURNAMENT OF ROSES PARADE

CASTLE GREEN APARTMENTS ▶
Built in 1898, this historic monument of Moorish design is one of the oldest co-operatives in the nation.

PASADENA CITY HALL ▶
Opened to the public in 1927, this award winning Palladian designed building is topped by a dome sheathed in copper. A cast iron fountain occupies its spacious courtyard.

PASADENA

Nestled against the foot of the San Gabriel Mountains to the east of Los Angeles, is Pasadena. Known for its historical homes, spectacular gardens, tree-lined avenues and the Norton Simon Museum of Art, Pasadena is the epitome of relaxation, respite, and retirement. That is, with the exception of New Years Day. For a solid week prior to the Rose Bowl football game on New Years Day, this low-key town turns into a cauldron of non-stop activity, its population abruptly swelling into a million and a half people, to watch the Tournament of Roses Parade. The streets are jam-packed with people from every place on earth. Camping on the sidewalks, or staying in motels, hotels, campers or trailers, this raucous horde of humanity infests this community each year to watch the armies of floats, festooned with millions of flowers, parade by majestically.

ABOUT THE ARTIST

When Dorothy Rice began painting the locales and people of Los Angeles, she embarked on one of the most exciting projects of her career.

Unlike many historical cities which have long-since seen their heyday, "grown-up" and settled down, Dorothy Rice saw Los Angeles still in the process of "becoming."

She packed up her materials, went to the streets, and started mingling with the people. She learned about them, their histories, and their feelings about Los Angeles. She sensed a freedom and easiness of life in Los Angeles that inspired her to express in watercolor and pen and ink, the feeling of this sprawling multi-cultural city. Each painting possesses its own texture, mood and style. Though the people, locales and architecture vary greatly, there is a subtle unity to her paintings. Whenever a particular scene moved her emotionally, she would set up her easel and paint on the spot, capturing that moment in time.

"**Painting to me is a search for the underlying values and the emotional illumination of the surroundings and people I encounter. The history of Los Angeles is living in its streets — the parks and beaches, and most of all, the history is being made today by the people and the life they have created around themselves. It's been three years of exploring, enjoying, and discovering. It can never be finished because Los Angeles is always changing.**"

Dorothy Rice studied at the Art Students League in New York City, the Otis/Parsons Art Institute, the Art Center College of Design in Los Angeles, and at the University of Guadalajara, Mexico.

Her one woman show of oils, "Serenata Mexicana" was such a great success at the prestigious Southwest Museum in Los Angeles, it was held over for two months. Westways Magazine featured Dorothy Rice's Mexican paintings in an illustrated three page article.

And, honored in a country renowned for its great muralists, Dorothy Rice is the only American artist ever invited to paint a mural at the University of Guadalajara in Mexico.

Dorothy Rice's oil and palate knife paintings are owned by many well known collectors and her current water color series is taking her around the world. Her work has been on exhibition in New York City, Tucson, in San Francisco at the Maxwell Gallery and in Los Angeles at the Many Horses Gallery. Her recent one woman shows at the Arco Center and the Upstairs Gallery in Los Angeles have created a great deal of excitement.

LOS ANGELES AIRPORT